New Vanguard • 121

Stryker Combat Vehicles

Gordon L Rottman · Illustrated by Hugh Johnson

First published in Great Britain in 2006 by Osprey Publishing, Midland House,
West Way, Botley, Oxford OX2 0PH, UK
443 Park Avenue South, New York, NY 10016, USA
E-mail: info@ospreypublishing.com

A CIP catalog record for this book is available from the British Library

ISBN 10: 1 84176 930 4
ISBN 13: 978 1 84176 930 1

Page layout by Melissa Orrom Swan, Oxford, UK
Index by Glyn Sutcliffe
Originated by The Electronic Page Company, UK
Printed in China through Worldprint Ltd

06 07 08 09 10   10 9 8 7 6 5 4 3 2 1

For a catalog of all books published by Osprey Military and Aviation
please contact:

NORTH AMERICA
Osprey Direct, c/o Random House Distribution Center, 400 Hahn Road,
Westminster, MD 21157
E-mail: info@ospreydirect.com

ALL OTHER REGIONS
Osprey Direct UK, P.O. Box 140 Wellingborough, Northants, NN8 2FA, UK
E-mail: info@ospreydirect.co.uk

www.ospreypublishing.com

Author's Acknowledgments

The author is indebted to Peter Keating of General Dynamics Land Systems,
Ken Caputo, Bob Cates, and Yves Bellanger.

ABBREVIATIONS

APC	Armored Personnel Carrier
ATGM	Antitank Guided Missile Vehicle
BFV	Bradley Fighting Vehicle (collective term for CFV and IFV)
C4ISR	Command, Control, Communications, Computer, Intelligence, Surveillance, and Reconnaissance
CFV	Cavalry Fighting Vehicle (Bradley)
CV	Command Vehicle
EPLRS	Enhanced Position-Locating Reporting System
ESV	Engineer Squad Vehicle
FBCB2	Force XXI Battle Command, Brigade-and-Below
FSV	Fire Support Vehicle
GDLS	General Dynamics Land Systems Division
HMMWV	High-Mobility Multi-Purpose Wheeled Vehicle ("Humvee" or "Hummer")
IAV	Interim Armored Vehicle
IBCT	Interim Brigade Combat Team
ICV	Infantry Carrier Vehicle
IED	Improvised Explosive Device
IFV	Infantry Fighting Vehicle (Bradley)
LAV	Light Armored Vehicle
MAV	Medium Armored Vehicle
MC	Mortar Carrier
MEV	Medical Evacuation Vehicle
MGS	Mobile Gun System
MOWAG	Motorwagenfabrik AG
NBC	Nuclear, Biological, and Chemical
NBCRV	NBC Reconnaissance Vehicle
RPG	Reaktivniy Protivotankoviy Granatomet – (rocket (propelled) antitank grenade)
rpm	rounds per minute
RSTA	Reconnaissance, Surveillance, and Target Acquisition
RV	Reconnaissance Vehicle
RWS	Remote Weapons Station
SBCT	Stryker Brigade Combat Team
TOW	Tube-launched, Optically tracked, Wire-guided missile

Artist's note

Readers may care to note that prints of the digital artwork from which the color
plates in this book were prepared are available for private sale. All reproduction
copyright whatsoever is retained by the Publishers. All inquiries should be
addressed to:

Hugh Johnson, 8 Bahram Road, Epsom, Surrey KT19 9DN, UK

The Publishers regret that they can enter into no correspondence upon
this matter.

STRYKER COMBAT VEHICLES

INTRODUCTION

The Stryker combat vehicle is the first major armored fighting vehicle (AFV) standardized by the US Army since the M1 Abrams tank in 1982. This controversial armored vehicle was fielded to fulfill a perceived need for a rapidly deployable AFV requiring a minimal logistical footprint, and enhanced by the latest technology.

One point regarding the Stryker should be clarified from the beginning. It was not designed to replace any existing combat vehicle. Stryker Brigade Combat Teams (SBCTs) were created as a new category of unit – a "medium force" – that did not previously exist. Stryker infantry carriers did not replace M113 Armored Personnel Carriers (APCs) or M2 Bradley Infantry Fighting Vehicles (IFVs), neither did the Stryker reconnaissance and antitank guided missile vehicles replace M3 Bradley Cavalry Fighting Vehicles (CFVs), nor did the Stryker mobile gun replace Abrams tanks. The Stryker augments existing forces to provide a more rapidly deployable medium contingency force. Only one mechanized brigade, previously in Korea, was converted to a SBCT. The other SBCTs were converted from light infantry brigades and the single wheeled-vehicle light armored cavalry regiment. One is also being formed from the assets of a mechanized infantry brigade in Germany, but the brigade will be reestablished in the United States. No other Abrams and Bradley-equipped heavy forces were lost with the activation of SBCTs.

A right front view of the Stryker M1126 Infantry Carrier Vehicle (ICV). Because of limited interior space, exterior equipment racks were fitted to the sides. The vertical wire-cutter bars can be seen on the front bow and forward of the weapons station. (GDLS)

WHEELED LIGHT ARMORED VEHICLES

For much of the 20th century, the US Army made only limited use of wheeled armored vehicles. Prior to World War II, a few types of machine-gun armed armored cars were in use, mainly by cavalry units. In 1942, however, a 6x6 light armored car – the M8 – was adopted by armored reconnaissance and tank destroyer units. The M8 mounted a turreted 37mm gun, while the variant M20 armored utility vehicle had an open compartment with a .50cal. machine gun. Both vehicles remained in use through the Korean War.

To allow infantry to support and keep pace with tanks in World War II, the US Army employed halftrack personnel carriers. Halftracks were provided to transport each rifle squad in armored rifle battalions, and they were also used as mortar carriers and command vehicles. These lightly armored vehicles, however, had only moderate cross-country ability and struggled to keep up with tanks. After World War II, therefore, development of full-tracked APCs began based on tank chassis. Yet it was not until the M59 was fielded in 1954 that a practical APC was provided to US mechanized forces, and in 1958 the revamped armored cavalry units were equipped with light tanks and full-tracked APCs. This trend continued through the 20th century, with armored cavalry squadrons becoming increasingly heavier – they had become combined arms maneuver units down to platoon level.

The M59 began to be replaced by the M113 APC series in the early 1960s. The M113 was a lighter, faster, amphibious vehicle that would be the mainstay US APC into the early 1990s, when it was completely replaced by the M2 Bradley IFV. In 1962 Cadillac Gage also began development of the V-100 Commando 4x4 armored car. A later version was purchased in 1965 as the M706 for use in convoy escort and airbase security in Vietnam. This

The 6x6 M8 Greyhound armored car served in cavalry reconnaissance and tank destroyer units through World War II and the Korean War. It was armed with a 37mm gun and .50cal. and .30cal. machine guns. (US Army)

evolved into the V-150 and was sold to foreign countries including Saudi Arabia and Panama. The 4x4 Cadillac Gage M1117 Guardian armored security vehicle, similar to the M706, was adopted for military police convoy escort in 1999.

The early postwar APCs were essentially "battle taxis." They carried infantrymen into battle, protecting them from small-arms fire, shell fragments, light mines, and nuclear, biological, and chemical (NBC) effects. They usually possessed one or two machine guns for offensive and defensive armament. The infantry passengers could not fight effectively from their carriers without opening overhead hatches and exposing themselves, plus the vehicle's interior, to any NBC contaminants. Other than the driver and vehicle commander, the passengers could not see the outside world. This prevented them from detecting close-in attacks and targets, and prohibited them from orienting the terrain and being familiar with it when dismounting. They charged out of the rear of the carrier into unfamiliar terrain with no idea of its layout, possible enemy locations, obstacles to avoid, or where they might find cover and concealment.

From the 1950s onwards the US Army was also almost totally focused on facing the Soviet threat on a European battlefield. The vehicle requirements were for heavy tanks capable of negotiating rugged terrain and rubble, large-caliber guns able to defeat correspondingly heavy tanks, advanced target acquisition, armor capable of withstanding most direct hits, and protection from NBC threats.

The Bradley M2 Fighting Vehicle (BFV) series, which included the M3 CFV, began fielding in the late 1970s, and remedied many of the deficiencies in APC design, while the M1 series Abrams tank met the Army's main battle tank requirements. Vehicles capable of keeping up with the Abrams were needed for the infantry and cavalry. The M2 IFV and M3 CFV met this need, and possessed the firepower to destroy their enemy counterparts and even tanks with their Tube-launched, Optically tracked, Wire-guided (TOW) missiles. They also had excellent cross-country abilities, reasonable armor protection, NBC defenses, and something earlier infantry tactical carriers did not provide, the ability to fight mounted. The BFV, however, has a high profile, higher than the M1 tank that it accompanies, and like any AFV the Bradley suffered teething problems alongside the Abrams. Yet regardless of the doomsayers' predictions, both vehicles performed extremely well in the

1990–91 Gulf War, dominating the Soviet-designed AFVs they had been intended to defeat. They continue to serve today. However, Bradleys are extremely expensive due to their advanced capabilities, and as a result few specialized support versions have been fielded, in contrast to the M113 where many variations were developed and deployed. M113-based mortar carriers, ambulances, antiarmor, fire support, smoke generator, air defense, command post vehicles, etc remain in use, as does the M113A3 as a utility vehicle.

By the late 1980s cavalry squadrons were equipped with Abrams tanks and Bradley CFVs and were more heavily armed than tank and mechanized infantry battalions. These units were employed as covering forces to attrite an advancing enemy, withdraw, and become a division counterattack force; a reconnaissance role was secondary. Meanwhile, the British made some use of wheeled armored vehicles, as did the West Germans, mainly for reconnaissance. The French employed light armored units equipped with heavy armored cars as well as infantry mounted in wheeled APCs and reconnaissance units with light armored cars. They found these units well suited for rapid overseas deployment, but they were only employed against poorly armed resistance in Africa and their use in the Gulf War, backed up by tanks and mechanized infantry, saw them facing only light opposition. In the United States, the M3 became the principal armored reconnaissance vehicle, but by the early 1990s it became apparent that stealth approaches were necessary, and at brigade and battalion levels the High-Mobility Multi-Purpose Wheeled Vehicle (HMMWV – "Humvee" or "Hummer") took over. Up-armored, armed HMMWVs have come into increasing use as infantry carriers, light combat, and escort vehicles since the end of the Cold War.[1]

ADOPTION OF THE STRYKER

Because of increasing tensions in Southwest Asia in the late 1970s, the US Army established the Rapid Deployment Task Force. It was recognized that

---

[1] See Osprey New Vanguard 122 *HMMWV Humvee 1980–2005: US Army Tactical Vehicle*, Steven J. Zaloga (Oxford, UK: Osprey Publishing, 2005)

heavy armor forces (68-ton Abrams and 33-ton Bradleys) would take too long to deploy, whether by ship or air. Sealift requires the armor to be moved to seaports with a time-consuming loading and transit time, and an unloading at an undeveloped seaport. While transit time is faster with airlift, the equipment is only piecemealed in and the aerial logistics tail cannot be sustained for long, therefore logistics also has to rely on sealift. Heavy armor requires a massive amount of fuel, repair parts, and maintenance equipment. For long intra-theater moves heavy full-tracked armor needs heavy equipment transporters as well as numerous cargo trucks to haul fuel, ammunition, spare parts, and support equipment. All these vehicles and materiel also have to be deployed into the theater and require their own support.

A more rapidly deployable and sustainable AFV was necessary. Light, full-tracked AFVs were lighter and required a bit less shipping space than heavy armor, but logistical support was still significant. The answer lay in wheeled armored vehicles. Primarily they were lighter, and far less demanding of fuel, maintenance, parts, and repair facilities. They could be off-loaded at poorly developed ports, were more easily loaded aboard ships and aircraft, and they could also travel long road distances on their own.

No vehicle in the inventory at this time could fulfill the requirement. In order to reduce development and procurement costs and to field units as rapidly as possible, it was decided to select and then adapt and develop an existing vehicle. Twenty manufacturers were asked to submit proposals in 1981. The choice was narrowed down to the British Alvis Stormer light full-tracked vehicle, Cadillac Gage V-150S four-wheeled armored car, Cadillac Gage V-300 six-wheeled armored car, and General Motors of Canada eight-wheeled Piranha light armored vehicle.

The Piranha was derived from the Swiss Motorwagenfabrik AG (MOWAG) armored car series in 6x6, 8x8, and 10x10 variants. The Piranha family included the 6x6 Grizzly APC, Cougar fire support vehicle, and Puma recovery vehicle used by Canada, as well as the 8x8 Bison. Over 5,000 Piranhas and variants such as the Marines' Light Armored Vehicle (LAV) family are in service worldwide with another

The Stryker was derived from the 8x8 Piranha III, variants of which are used by a couple of dozen countries. Here are Australian ASLAV-25s deployed to southern Iraq and in use since 1996. (Ken Caputo)

3d Brigade, 2d Infantry Division, infantrymen repair a tire damaged by gunfire. The soldier in the foreground is armed with an M4 carbine mounting a 40mm M203A1 grenade launcher. (US Army)

3,000 on order, making the family one of the most widely used AFV series today.[2] The Piranha was selected as the basis for the new M1047 LAV in 1982 and almost 1,000 were ordered, mostly for the US Army. The 8x8 amphibious LAV family included a full range of vehicles from the basic LAV-25 fitted with the same 25mm chain-gun turret as the Bradley, to the antitank vehicle (LAV-AT) mounting twin TOW tubes, mortar carrier (LAV-M) with an 81mm mortar, command-and-control vehicle (LAV-C2), logistics vehicle (LAV-L), recovery vehicle (LAV-R), air defense vehicle (LAV-AD) with a 25mm rotary cannon and eight Stinger missiles, and the Mobile Electronic Warfare Support System (MEWSS). A 105mm assault gun (LAV-105) was envisioned, but developmental and funding problems precluded its adoption.

In 1984 Congress withdrew the Army's LAV funding when it was decided that the HMMWV would meet its requirements. The Marines continued with the program and raised four LAV battalions in 1983–85 using the Army LAVs. The LAV battalion was mainly a reconnaissance unit, but it could be employed to mobilize infantry, as a LAV-25 has space for six passengers. The LAV battalions did not possess any organic dismount troops, however, and in 1988 they began to convert to light armored infantry (LAI) battalions and received dismountable scouts. In 1992, as a result of the lessons learned during Operation *Desert Storm*, the LAI battalions began to be reorganized as reconnaissance battalions (light armored) and then officially became light armored reconnaissance (LAR) battalions in 1994.

The LAV was successfully employed during contingency operations in Panama, Kuwait, Somalia, Haiti, Kosovo, Afghanistan, and Iraq. These operations ranged from shows of force, peacekeeping, counterinsurgency and security operations, through to conventional warfare. They were seen deployed in deserts, rolling plains, forests, and urban areas. The Marines were pleased with their performance and continued to procure variants.

---

2 They are used by Austria, Canada, Chile (which also builds them), Denmark, Ghana, Ireland, New Zealand, Nigeria, Oman, Saudi Arabia, Switzerland, and the United States, as well as other countries in smaller numbers.

The LAV eventually saw use by the Army. Prior to the Gulf War the 82d Airborne Division borrowed 14 LAV-25s and a LAV-R as reconnaissance vehicles from the Marines for 3d Battalion (Airborne), 73d Armor, which was equipped with Sheridan M551A1 air-droppable tanks. The LAVs had to be modified for loading aboard C-130s and the Army was less than pleased with their cross-country performance, so returned them to the Marines after the war.

The Army, in light of the traditional Soviet threat, had little interest in expending scarce funds on wheeled AFVs. However, this situation would soon change. In the spring of 1999, when the air war was launched against Serbia over abuses in Kosovo, the Army attempted to deploy Task Force Hawk. The force had only to deploy from central Germany to Tirana, Albania, by airlift – a distance of 1,290km (800 miles). The situation at Tirana was deplorable owing to lack of space for arriving units and supplies, overcrowding with refugees, and mud and rain. Another problem was the bloated 5,000-man task force, whose main goal was to deploy Apache attack helicopters for use in neighboring Kosovo, as well as Multiple Launch Rocket System (MLRS) units. Bradley and Abrams units were used for security and to provide the basis for a ground combat force that the Army expected to commit. Excessive command-and-control assets were included to prepare for the arrival of additional forces, as well as a large logistics tail to sustain the diversified force. Yet the war was over before Task Force Hawk could fully deploy, causing Madeleine Albright, the then US UN Ambassador, to say, "What's the use of having the world's best military when you don't get to use them?" The debacle was a great embarrassment for the Army. Some in Congress questioned whether the Army was strategically relevant, and whether it could even effectively deploy to future trouble spots on a timely basis and sustain itself. This controversy partly arose because Task Force Hawk was also an inappropriate type of force for that kind of war.

General Eric K. Shinseki was appointed US Army Chief of Staff in June 1999 and began to transform the Army for the 21st century. While

An ICV of Company A, 5th Battalion, 20th Infantry Regiment, 2d Infantry Division, at Yakima Training Center, WA. The squad leader has emerged from his hatch aft of the driver's station. Concertina wire coils are stowed on the bow. There are 14 M2 IFVs and an M113A3 APC in a Bradley rifle company. A Stryker rifle company has 14 ICVs, three MGSs, two MCs, an FSV, and an MEV. Both companies have two HMMWVs and two 2 1/2-ton trucks, all with trailers. (US Army)

The German-built 6x6 M93A1 Fox NBC reconnaissance system is presently used in lieu of the M1135 NBCRV, which will be fielded later. The 17-ton Fox is amphibious and crewed by three personnel. This one is painted in the NATO three-color European camouflage scheme. (US Army)

Desert Storm proved that the US could deploy significant heavy forces to the Middle East, it had taken months to build up the force, and it was felt that this luxury of time could not be afforded in future international conflicts. Heavy forces – the "Legacy Force" (heavy armor and mechanized forces) – were still necessary, but a more rapidly deployable and easily sustainable "Interim Force"[3] was also required. This new medium force might not be able to deal with enemy heavy forces, but the capability was needed to deploy some kind of maneuver force more rapidly than the months required for a heavy force. The Interim Force was intended to tackle light forces and insurgents. Shinseki wanted the capability to deploy a Brigade Combat Team (BCT) anywhere in the world within 96 hours and a division in 120 hours. This new unit was initially called the Interim Brigade Combat Team (IBCT).

The IBCT could be preceded by a forced-entry force of paratroopers and/or Special Operations Forces (SOF) and had to be sufficiently light to allow rapid air deployment into a region with an austere logistical infrastructure, as well as being highly maneuverable and possessing considerable firepower. To give the IBCT an edge, its command, control, communications, and intelligence capabilities would rely on advanced technology. It would be equipped with a then undetermined wheeled light armored vehicle called the Interim Armored Vehicle (IAV) as it was not thought that this would be the final wheeled AFV to eventually equip the Objective Force. It was also sometimes referred to as the Medium Armored Vehicle (MAV).

DEVELOPMENT OF THE STRYKER

As with the LAV, it was decided that the IAV would have to be selected from off-the-shelf vehicles. Eleven firms sent candidate vehicles to Ft. Knox, KY,

---

3 The long-term goal is to field an "Objective Force" by 2010. It is to possess Future Combat System (FCS) vehicles weighing just below 40,000lbs which are transportable in C-130s and have the lethality and survivability of the Abrams.

The rear of an ICV displays the drop ramp with its inset troop door, fuel (left)/water (right) can racks, and "air-guard" hatches above the ramp. The web straps forward of the top hatches are for securing ammunition cans. The circular air-vent can be seen centered in the ammunition rack. (GDLS)

at the end of 1999, which included infantry carriers and some specialized variants. A few light-tracked vehicles were also submitted, but most were wheeled. The vehicles undertook live-fire and cross-country driving demonstrations. Some developmental vehicles were for display only. The purpose of the Platform Performance Demonstration was not to select a vehicle, but to exhibit capabilities and available technology.

Amid accusations of pre-selection and serious doubts over the wisdom of the selection, the choice of the 8x8 LAV III, built by the teamed General Motors of Canada and General Dynamics Land Systems Division (GDLS), was announced on November 16, 2000. The LAV III was already used by the Canadian Army and had a reputation for reliability. It was a version of the Piranha III built by MOWAG (now part of GDLS-Europe), and while similar in appearance to the Marine LAV, the LAV III was larger and readily adaptable to most planned variants.

On February 27, 2002, at the Association of the US Army Conference in Washington, DC, the Army formally named the new vehicle family after two posthumous Medal of Honor winners, Private First Class Stuart Stryker serving with 2d Battalion, 513th Parachute Infantry, 13th Airborne Division in World War II, and Specialist 4 Robert Stryker, a grenadier with 1st Battalion, 26th Infantry, 1st Infantry Division in Vietnam.[4]

The Army committed itself to spend $4 billion to purchase 2,131 Strykers over six years. Engineering takes place in Sterling Heights, MI, upper hull assembly in Lima, OH, and structure fabrication and final assembly in Anniston, AL, and London, Ontario (Canada). In all some 20 firms (four foreign) and two US Army arsenals are involved in producing components and systems for the Strykers. The adoption of the Stryker led to the cancellation of the M9 Armored Gun System (AGS). This was a 105mm gun-armed full-tracked light tank, which was to have

---

4 This was only the second time a vehicle was officially named after enlisted men. The first was the 1980s problem-plagued Sergeant York air defense vehicle, which was canceled.

One of the main issues with the Stryker is that it cannot be carried fully combat-loaded or configured when airlifted aboard a C-130 transport. Only half of the carrier's squad can fly on the same aircraft. Here an ICV off-loads from a C-130H. (US Army)

replaced the aging M551A1 Sheridan tanks of the 82d Airborne Division's 1st Battalion (Airborne), 73d Armor, and would have been provided to the 2d Armored Cavalry Regiment (Light).[5]

The design requirements called for adaptation of the basic vehicle to ten variants, although some would require extensive redesign. Keeping the basic vehicle layout was essential in order to reduce spare parts stocks, maintenance equipment, and specialty trained mechanics, and to simplify crew training.

Strykers have a self-recovery capability to extract themselves from mud, ditches, etc in the form of a hydraulic winch. The vehicle acoustic (engine and exhaust noise) and thermal (engine and exhaust heat) signatures are less than those of the Bradley. Noise reduction is further improved by the use of wheels rather than tracks. Armor protection standards require integral all-around 14.5mm armor-piercing-incendiary and artillery airburst protection. The vehicle must be upgradeable to rocket-propelled grenade (RPG) protection by some form of add-on armor.

Three block improvements are planned for the Stryker: a crew-installable add-on armor kit providing 360-degree RPG protection, an internally mounted 120mm mortar for the MC, and embedded training programs in the on-board computer. Each block of Strykers built for each SBCT contains improvements over earlier blocks, but upgrade kits are provided for the earlier vehicles.

The lightweight Stryker allows a maximum road speed of 96.5kph (62.5mph). Most tracked AFVs are slower and the maximum speed varies between the different types. This means a tracked AFV column can maintain a 40kph (25mph) speed with 8–24kph (5–15mph) additional speed if necessary. A Stryker column can achieve 64–72kph (40–45mph) with 24–32kph (15–20mph) extra speed if required. This capability allows for more rapid intra-theater deployment, and a higher speed also improves dash ability for darting from cover-to-cover.

5 The 2d ACR was the XVIII Airborne Corps' HMMWV-mounted reconnaissance unit.

Three Strykers, here an ICV, can be carried aboard a C-17A transport. Unlike the tight-fitting C-130, here there is ample room on the sides to allow loadmasters access to check tie-down chains. "Bumper numbers" on Strykers are commonly black on sand-colored rectangles. This is vehicle number 11 in Company A. The "2I-1-23I" translates as "2d Infantry Division, 1st Battalion, 23d Infantry Regiment." (US Army)

All Strykers and the SBCT as an entity are fully integrated through a high-technology system, the Command, Control, Communications, Computer, Intelligence, Surveillance, and Reconnaissance (C4ISR) capability. All variants must be transportable in the C-130E/H Hercules The C-130 and C-17 can land on remote, rudimentary airstrips; the C5A Galaxy, which could not, was phased out in 2005. A C-130 can carry one Stryker and a C-17 three. It is expected that the revamped MGS will have to be carried two per C-17. The ability to deploy quickly is the reason that a wheeled LAV was adopted – it is also one of the main bones of contention for Stryker opponents. The Stryker's weight and bulk are barely within airlift parameters, which include the requirement for the vehicle to be disembarked combat-ready. The Stryker infantry carrier's weight is 36,240lbs while a C-130H normally carries 38,000lbs – most combat-loaded Stryker variants exceed this slightly. They can still be carried, but the C-130's 1,383km (860-mile) range is reduced. The Stryker's bulk is such that the US Air Force issued a temporary waiver on the 14in safety aisle around all sides of a vehicle that allows loadmasters to inspect tie-downs and give them unhindered access to all parts of the aircraft.

While opponents claimed that the Stryker was not air-droppable, this has proved untrue. In August 2004 the Air Force dropped a 52,500lb MGS from a C-17A using 10 x 100ft parachutes. Hopefully the 82d Airborne Division will eventually be provided MGSs to replace its inactivated light tank battalion. Other variants may also be airdropped.

To load a Stryker aboard an aircraft its height-management system is used to lower its height by reducing tire pressure. The Remote Weapons Station (RWS) is folded down, and some equipment items and ammunition are re-stowed or removed to meet restrictions. Only a half-full fuel tank is permitted. Radio antennas, left-rear water can mount, two upper smoke grenade launchers, bow wire-cutter, and the wheel bump stop between the second and third wheels are removed and no crew equipment may be stowed on the exterior. Only half of the accompanying squad can ride aboard the aircraft. Other Stryker variants require similar reconfiguration. The vehicle can be off-loaded in three minutes, after the tie-downs have been removed, which requires several minutes. It takes just under 20 minutes to reconfigure the vehicle for combat, although time is required for the rest of the squad to link-up from another aircraft and for additional fuel and ammunition to be loaded. Admittedly it is rare for a unit to go into action immediately upon landing. Expeditionary airfields able to accept transports are rarely on the frontline and would have been already secured by paratroopers or SOF. Permitting up to an hour to ready a Stryker is not unrealistic.

The prototype of the Stryker 105mm mobile gun is far too heavy and bulky for transport in a C-130 and major modifications are underway. The Stryker antitank vehicle also has height problems. Most other vehicles assigned to Stryker brigades can be loaded in C-130s with the exception of the Heavy Expanded Mobility Tactical Truck (HEMTT) fuelers and wreckers and Fox NBC reconnaissance vehicles.

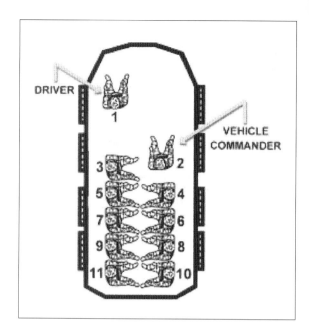

The seating arrangement of an ICV carrying a rifle squad. The squad leader (or platoon leader) is the number 3 figure. (US Army)

STRYKER DESCRIBED

Stryker comprises two main variants, the Infantry Carrier Vehicle (ICV) (699) and the Mobile Gun System (MGS) (238). (The figures given in parenthesis are the planned total procurement numbers.) The ICV has eight additional configurations: Reconnaissance Vehicle (RV) (393), Mortar Carrier (MC) (224), Command Vehicle (CV) (112), Fire Support Vehicle (FSV) (108), Engineer Squad Vehicle (ESV) (76), Medical Evacuation Vehicle (MEV) (114), Antitank Guided Missile Vehicle (ATGM) (88), and Nuclear, Biological, and Chemical Reconnaissance Vehicle (NBCRV) (44). Eight configurations are now in production. The MGS and NBCRV are still undergoing development and will be delivered in 2006. While the Stryker variants are designated by model numbers, they are commonly known by their abbreviations.

The basic Stryker ICV weighs approximately 38,000lbs combat loaded.[6] Its length is 22ft 11in, width 8ft 11in, and height 8ft 8in exclusive of the weapons mounting. The vehicle is divided into two main compartments each occupying approximately half the hull and separated by a firewall. The forward portion contains the diesel engine on the right side with the transmission forward. The exhaust vent is on the forward right side on the edge of the upper deck and the engine air intake is on the left behind the driver's compartment. The hydraulic winch is in the center bow with a port provided for the cable and an access hatch to the left. The driver compartment is on the left side over the gap between the first and second axles – access/egress is through an overhead rectangular hatch and a passage connected to the troop compartment.

The commander's station is in the right front of the rear troop compartment over the third axle and the RWS is located just forward of the

---

6 The variant vehicle and total combat load weights provided here were produced at the National Training Center in 2003. The average weight of the variants, exclusive of the MGS, was 37,988lbs and a combat loaded weight of 39,144lbs.

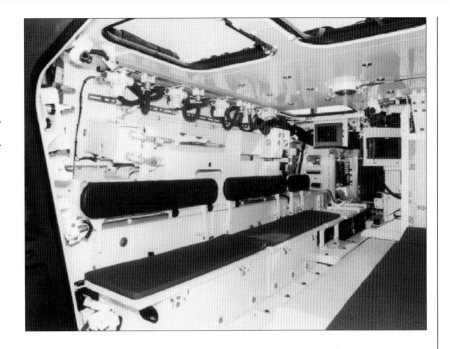

ICV's circular commander's hatch. Crew/passenger seating arrangements differ between variants. In the hull's rear is a powered drop-type ramp, the primary means of access/egress. A small door opening to the right is set in the center of the ramp. To the left of the commander's hatch is a rectangular troop hatch. Two similar hatches are positioned side-by-side on the rear end of the deck and open outward. These three "air-guard" hatches provide emergency access/egress as well as allowing soldiers to observe and engage targets. This action of course necessitates the soldiers exposing their heads and shoulders. There are no hull vision or firing ports. There is a small square "bailout" hatch on the left side below the forward top hatch and above the third and fourth wheels.

External fittings include headlights, blackout drive, turn indicator, brake lights, lifting and towing rings, antenna mountings, camouflage net poles, and hand-tool racks. On either side are equipment storage racks for ammunition and 5gal (20 liter) water and fuel cans and to the left and right of the rear ramp are racks for two 5gal cans. The side and rear racks together hold 20 x 5gal cans. Fitted forward of the driver's hatch is a hinged vertical wire-cutter bar protecting exposed crew/passengers from downed telephone/power lines. Another wire-cutter may be mounted atop the forward portion of the deck depending on armament arrangement. Most variants have a mounting for a 7.62mm M240B machine gun forward of the commander's hatch.

Mobility and automotive

The Stryker can achieve a top speed of 96.5kph (62.5mph) and can accelerate to 80kph (50mph) in eight seconds. Range is 532km (330 miles) at 64kph (40mph). The engine, mounted in the front to improve vehicle survivability and maximize crew/passenger space in the rear, is a diesel Caterpillar 3126 developing 350hp at 2,500rpm. This same engine is used in the medium tactical vehicle family (cargo trucks) and the interchange-ability further reduces logistics needs. The engine has six speeds forward

and one in reverse, with a two-speed transfer case and four automotive differentials (the Allison MD 3066P automatic transmission is used). An air-conditioning unit may be added beside the engine, but this is standard only in the CV. Two fuel tanks, together containing 53gals (200 liters), are in external armored sponsons on either side of the ramp on the hull's lower rear end. If one tank is penetrated the fuel supply can be switched to the other and the vehicle continues. While the engine is diesel, the Army's primary fuel is JP8, a jet engine fuel slightly less combustible than diesel. A Mechron 28.5-volt auxiliary power unit provides DC power for systems operation and 24-volt battery charging when the engine is off.

The eight wheels have independent hydro-pneumatic suspension, with a height-management system allowing it to be raised up to 9in for more ground clearance or lowered for loading aboard aircraft. This system is also self-correcting and can adjust the vehicle's balance depending on terrain and vehicle position.

The central tire inflation system has four pre-selected tire pressures: road, terrain, sand, and emergency. Tire pressure is automatically adjusted every 30 seconds, decreasing tire pressure for reduced ground pressure on soft ground. The driver can re-inflate the tires without halting when the vehicle gains firm ground. Four of the wheels are permanently powered and the other four when desired. The front four wheels can be steered. The Michelin 1200R20 XML tires have Hutchinson run-flat liners and reports from Iraq state that vehicles have maintained full-speed and maneuverability with all tires shredded by gunfire and RPGs. All eight wheels have air-power brakes with antilock brake systems (ABS) on the rear three axles.

The Stryker can cross a 6ft 6in wide trench, climb a 1ft 11in vertical obstacle, negotiate a 60 percent forward slope and a 30 percent side slope. It requires a 17m turning radius. A major departure from past tactical infantry carriers is that the Stryker is not amphibious, but can ford a 3ft 6in depth, 5ft with preparation.

Troops of 3d Brigade, 2d Infantry Division, dismount from their ICV. Stryker infantrymen operate akin to dragoons. They ride into combat and can fight mounted, but intend to fight dismounted whenever necessary. (US Army)

Protective measures

Armor protection has been a major criticism of the Stryker. The vehicle is not as well protected as the Bradley. While some call for the use of the M113, it only offers protection from 7.62mm armor-piercing and marginal protection from .50cal. Armor offering 14.5mm protection for the M113 has been developed, but never fielded.

The Stryker hull is made of 1/2in high-hardness steel capable of defeating 7.62mm. This is backed by a Kevlar® spall liner. The sloped frontal and side armor aid in protection; the M113 mostly has vertical armor. Modular EXpandable Armor System (MEXAS 2) ceramic appliqué armor can be added that protects against 14.5mm, although this is not normally fixed to the vehicle during training as it adds over 7,000lbs. In October 2001 the German-made ceramic armor was tested and found deficient – the chemical content was changed by the manufacturer without notifying the Army, therefore the new tiles were not certified as bullet resistant. X-rays after test firing showed the tiles had been weakened by the impacts. Some tiles were of a different size than the approved tiles and others were made by unapproved sub-contractors. A denser ceramic armor was provided in May 2002 now backed by 3mm steel plates and offering protection from 14.5mm rounds. Up to 126 ceramic tiles are applied depending on the Stryker variant, and when this armor is added the Stryker's weight is increased to 43,000lbs, preventing it being carried in a C-130. Ceramic armor, while twice as effective as rolled homogeneous armor, will fail after multiple hits.

A major threat exists for AFVs in the form of the Russian-designed RPG-7 (rocket-propelled grenade). In November 2002 a contract was let for the development of RPG-proof ceramic appliqué armor, and 1,600 retrofit kits are to be delivered in 2006. This armor will add considerable weight to the Stryker and also increase its width.

A stop-gap RPG armor is the slat armor cage fitted to all Strykers in Iraq. This is a frame of horizontal bars fitted to mounting brackets surrounding the vehicle, called "birdcage armor" by the troops. It is similar in principle to the bar armor that was fitted to riverine craft in Vietnam for protection from the same weapon. RPG shaped-charge warheads striking one of the

Here shown in Iraq, this ICV is fitted with the controversial slat armor. While the armor adds a great deal of weight, adversely affecting its off-road capability and making it top heavy with increased roll-over hazard, it has proved to be effective against RPG fire. (US Army)

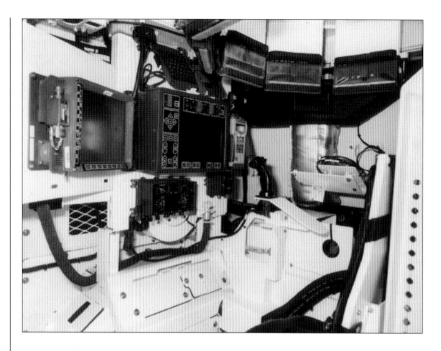

The Stryker vehicle commander's station with the driver's thermal imaging vision enhancer monitor and the Remote Weapons Station's (RWS) Video Display Terminal monitor to the right. Some of the seven M45 periscopes surrounding his overhead hatch can be seen. (GDLS)

slats detonate a sufficient distance from the vehicle's body to prevent penetration. A warhead striking between two slats will short out its piezoelectric-detonating system and break up without exploding. Several problems owing to weight and bulk are caused by slat armor and these are discussed in Plate G. It does, however, offer effective protection: the second SBCT in Iraq sustained over 250 RPG attacks in six months with 70 direct hits and the slat armor prevented any from penetrating.

Explosive reactive armor is under development for the Stryker. This consists of brick-like explosive charges bolted to the body; they detonate when struck by a shaped-charge projectile and disperse its penetrating blast. Yet these too add excessive weight and width. They are also hazardous to dismounted infantrymen within 100m, making reactive armor impractical for personnel carriers.

Overhead protection is resistant to air-bursting 152mm rounds, the underside is protected from light antitank mines, and the vision blocks and periscopes resist 7.62mm bullets. The ICV's RWS, with its sensitive optics and sensors, is vulnerable to small-arms fire. Regardless of the type of armor, the wheel wells cannot be protected by additional armor and are a rather vulnerable area.

NBC protection is provided by on-board detectors and a ventilation system into which protective masks are plugged. Automatically activated halogen fire suppression systems are fitted with a one-shot in the troop compartment and a two-shot for the engine.

C4ISR

As previously discussed, Strykers are outfitted with extensive state-of-the-art Command, Control, Communications, Computer, Intelligence, Surveillance, and Reconnaissance (C4ISR) systems. Secure communications are provided by SINgle-Channel Ground and Airborne Radio System (SINCGARS – "Sing-gars") sets, through which the driver/commander intercom operates. Depending on a given vehicle's function and echelon it

The vehicle commander's station with its seat, RWS control joystick, and automatic fire extinguishers. Stryker interiors are painted acrylic glossy white. (GDLS)

can mount one to four radios of different models plus one or two portable radios for dismounted use. Other equipment includes the AN/TSQ-158 Enhanced Position-Locating Reporting System (EPLRS), an AN/PSN-11 Precise Lightweight GPS Receiver/Defense Advanced GPS Receiver (PLGR/DAGR – "Pluger"), and the Video Display Terminal (VDT). The latter is a monitor displaying the view seen by the video camera on the RWS' thermal imager camera.

The Force XXI Battle Command, Brigade-and-Below system (FBCB2) is an AN/YUK-128 computer used by leaders/commanders at all echelons on the communications network. It is mounted at the vehicle commander's station and is a digital system allowing communication between vehicles through text messaging and a map network, a "tactical Internet." The digital map displays the position of all vehicles and any user can mark enemy elements and positions on the map when they have been detected. The FBCB2 relies on the EPLRS to provide a computer-controlled communications network transmitting digital data, position location, and reporting. A commander or staff officer at any echelon can access the tactical data and element locations of the units under his control, plus those of higher units and adjacent units, to immediately coordinate tactical operations, all forms of fire support, and support logistical activities. Friendly unit locations and actions are immediately transmitted, as is intelligence information. Units and information not of interest to a particular leader can be filtered out.

The commander's station has seven M45 periscopes around the cupola, but with a blind quadrant to the right rear. The driver has three M17 periscopes and an AN/VAS-5 thermal imaging driver's vision enhancer with a digital camera, allowing him to drive in poor visibility with hatches closed. Monitors display this view to the vehicle commander and squad leader.

STRYKER VARIANTS

M1126 Infantry Carrier Vehicle (ICV)

The ICV is designed to carry a nine-man squad and two-man crew, the crew being a driver and a vehicle commander who doubles as the gunner. There are inward-facing bench seats on either side of the troop compartment seating four on the right and five on the left. The squad leader sits on the forward end of the left bench to the left of the vehicle commander. The squad leader can use the overhead hatch to the left of the vehicle commander's to look outside the vehicle. He has no periscope. His vision to the right front is restricted by the RWS and he must duck inside if the weapon is fired to the left.

One of the criticisms of the ICV is that infantrymen cannot see outside, much less fire their weapons, denying the squad effective situational awareness of what is going on externally and the lay of the terrain when they dismount. They do have a restricted view of the outside world via the VDT linked to the RWS and the driver's enhanced imager camera (this is mainly for the squad leader's use).

The RWS Video Display Terminal (VDT) at the vehicle commander's station. This monitor displays the view seen by the RWS' video thermal imager camera. (US Army)

Another drawback of the ICV is that it is not provided with more potent armament capable of defeating enemy light AFVs, as its primary role is an infantry carrier and not a mounted combat vehicle. The squad can fight from the ICV, but the vehicle is not meant to stand up against heavier AFVs. The ICV's primary armament, either a .50cal. M2 machine gun or a 40mm Mk 19 Mod 3 automatic grenade launcher, is mounted on the "Protector" XM151 RWS built by Vinghog AS of Norway. The system allows the gunner (vehicle commander) to acquire and engage targets around 360 degrees using a monitor screen. The RWS was initially not stabilized, but stabilization is being retrofitted, allowing the gun to be fired accurately on the move. The RWS is also fitted with an infrared sensor, laser rangefinder, and thermal imager camera with video recorder. This zoomable camera has a 45-degree field of vision and can be magnified up to x30. Four four-tube M6 smoke grenade launchers[7] are mounted on the RWS. A tripod is provided for the weapon if it is dismounted. In c.2015 both weapons may be replaced by the 25mm XM307 Objective Crew Served Weapon (OCSW). A 7.62mm M240B machine gun can be mounted externally to be fired from the commander's hatch. Ammunition storage includes:

40mm	430 rounds or
.50cal.	2,000
7.62mm	3,200
5.56mm carbine	2,240
5.56mm SAW	1,120
Smoke grenades	32
Javelins	4

The 40mm grenade launcher has a rate of fire of 325–375rpm (40–60rpm practical rate) with a maximum effective range of 1,500m using high-explosive and dual-purpose (shaped-charge/fragmentation) high-explosive. The .50cal. machine gun has a 450–600rpm rate of fire to an effective range of 1,200m. The ICV weighs 37,630lbs with a combat loaded weight of 39,940lbs.

---

7 The M6 fires British-designed 66mm L8A1/A3 red phosphorus grenades some 30m, which burst with dense white smoke clouds to screen vehicles as they withdraw.

A Stryker rifle squad loads gear aboard its IFV. A squad consists of the squad leader, two fire-team leaders, two squad automatic weapon (SAW) gunners, two grenadiers, a designated marksman, and an antiarmor specialist, in addition to the two-man ICV crew. (US Army)

M1127 Reconnaissance Vehicle (RV)

The RV is supplied to the Reconnaissance, Surveillance, and Target Acquisition (RSTA) troops' platoons and infantry battalion scout platoons. Apart from the two-man crew the RV carries a five-man reconnaissance team and it mounts a .50cal. on a cupola. As well as operating as a reconnaissance vehicle, the RV is also used for conducting dismounted reconnaissance actions. The vehicle can deliver the scout team a safe distance from the objective and the team reconnoiters, relaying information back to the hidden vehicle. This deployment method allows the scout team to use lightweight radios and carry only minimal gear. Mounted beside the commander's hatch is the Long-Range Advanced Scout Surveillance System (LRAS3) pod, a real-time acquisition, target detection, recognition, identification, and far-target location collection system. It has standoff, all-weather collection sensors including forward-looking infrared thermal imager, a day video camera, laser rangefinder, long-range common aperture reflective optics, and a GPS interferometer subsystem. The LRAS3 interfaces with the FBCB2 system. The RV weighs 37,090lbs with a loaded weight of 38,350lbs.

The M1127 Reconnaissance Vehicle (RV) mounts an LRAS3 pod to the right of the vehicle commander's hatch alongside the .50cal. machine gun. Many of the pilot vehicles had the large tow rings on the bow and rear painted silver and secured by red bolts. On fielded Strykers these are painted green. (GDLS)

M1128 Mobile Gun System (MGS)

By far the most controversial Stryker is the MGS. The prototypes are extremely heavy – 52,500lbs – overly top heavy, and too high profiled to carry in a C-130, even though the hull is lowered 6in. They have to be deployed by C-17s. There are also limitations on the direction the gun can be fired – for example, if fired to the side when the MGS is on a side slope it might roll over. The Marines experienced similar problems developing the LAV-105, which was canceled.

The MGS mounts a British-designed 105mm M68A1E4 gun as previously used on the M1, M60A3, and M48A5 tanks. Its effective range is almost 2,000m at 6rpm. The low-profile turret is unmanned; the gunner is inside the hull.

An 18-round automatic loader reduces height and while the auto-loader is heavy, the small turret reduces weight. The MGS mounts a .50cal. at the commander's hatch, a coaxial M240C, and two M6 grenade launchers served by a three-man crew. The 105mm rounds include various types of armor-piercing discarding sabot-tracer, high-explosive antitank-tracer (shaped-charge), and white phosphorus tracer, and a canister round is under development. Ammunition load is 30 rounds of 105mm, 400 rounds of .50cal., and 3,400 rounds of 7.62mm.

The MGS will provide the rifle company with not only an antitank capability, but a direct fire support gun to attack bunkers and fortified buildings, something the infantry has lacked. The ATGM is currently substituted for the MGS. The first eight pre-production MGSs were delivered in July 2002. Extensive redesign is necessary to reduce weight, with a target of 41,000lbs, but it is doubtful that this will be achieved: even the internal winch was removed without having any real impact. The reworked MGS was to be delivered in September 2005, but was delayed until August 2006. Canada, also desiring light deployable forces, is replacing its German Leopard C2 tanks with the MGS.

The M1128 Mobile Gun System (MGS). A .50cal. M2 machine gun is mounted at the commander's hatch to the left of the gun. The MGS is plagued by problems of excessive weight and top-heaviness. (GDLS)

M1129 Mortar Carrier (MC)

The MC-A is the current mortar carrier. It is sometimes called the "MCV," but MC is the correct abbreviation. The MC-A carries two mortars internally. They cannot be fired from within the MC, but are dismounted and set-up on the ground. All MCs carry an Israeli-designed 120mm M120 mortar with 60 rounds of high-explosive, white phosphorus smoke, illumination, precision-guided, and dual-purpose improved conventional munitions (cluster munitions). Rifle company mortar squads also carry a 60mm M224 mortar for use if operating on foot without vehicle support. The battalion mortar squads have a British-designed 81mm M252 mortar for the same purpose. RSTA squadron MCs do not carry a second mortar. If operating without vehicle support the four-man crew, which includes the MC crew, must be augmented to man-pack adequate ammunition. The MC-A is fitted with a RWS with a .50cal. and weighs 38,940lbs, with a loaded weight of 39,990lbs.

Mortar	Range
60mm M224	3,490m
81mm M252	7,700m
120mm M120/M121	7,240m

The MC-B began replacing the MC-A in August 2005 in 3d Brigade, 2d Infantry Division – the MC-B had been tested earlier, but a September 2004 assessment recommended further development to improve reliability and safety. This vehicle has a large two-piece top hatch that allows the mortar to be fired from inside the carrier. The rear compartment is also wider, and the 120mm M121 mortar is fitted on a 360-degree turntable mount. A planned 81mm variant was canceled.

M1130 Command Vehicle (CV)

The CV is provided to commanders from battalion to brigade levels as well as reconnaissance troops. It has a crew of two and can seat four passengers – an additional seat was added after the CV was introduced. The numbers and types of radios depend on the type of unit and its echelon.

An M1129B Mortar Carrier (MC-B) showing the 120mm M121 mortar on its 360-degree turntable. The muzzle attenuator device reduces muzzle blast. The mortar can be fired with the rear ramp closed, but it is better opened to reduce blast overpressure and to allow ammunition to be passed from the 1 1/2-ton trailer to conserve ready ammunition in the internal side racks. The MC-A was essentially a modified ICV carrying a 120mm M120 mortar that could only be fired dismounted. (US Army)

An M1130 Command Vehicle (CV) carries commanders at battalion and higher echelons. It mounts numerous radios and command-and-control systems. This CV has a 40mm automatic grenade launcher on its RWS, but it is usually fitted with a .50cal. machine gun. (GDLS)

Other equipment includes the Lightweight Video Reconnaissance System II (LVRS), a man-portable camera able to transmit still images over radios. The CV is fitted with a Delphi air conditioner, armament is a RWS with a .50cal., and it weighs 36,660lbs with a total loaded weight of 38,130lbs.

M1131 Fire Support Vehicle (FSV)

The FSV is provided to the RSTA squadron to acquire, identify, and report distant targets to the artillery battalion and the mortar elements in the RSTA squadron and infantry battalions. The Fire Support Sensor System (FS3) provides an AN/TAS-4B thermal imager/day camera, laser rangefinder, and AN/TVQ-2 laser locator designator for use with laser-guided smart munitions. (The FS3's pedestal and pod are mounted in place of the left forward deck hatch.) Its FBCB2 provides information on friendly unit locations to prevent friendly fire incidents and presents known enemy locations as detected by all other units. Targeting data collected by the FSV is shared with all other SBCT elements through four radio nets. The vehicle has a four-man crew and is armed with a .50cal. on a cupola. It weighs 37,220lbs with a loaded weight of 37,850lbs. The FSV was not fielded until May 2003.

M1132 Engineer Squad Vehicle (ESV)

The ESV (often miscalled an engineer "support" vehicle) provides the squad not only with mobility and protection, but serves as an obstacle-breaching vehicle. Besides the nine-man squad it also carries a two-man crew. The squad is armed as the rifle squad, but lacks a Javelin antiarmor system. Armament is a RWS with a .50cal. The ESV can mount a bulldozer-like mine-plow or mine-roller, and it weighs 38,450lbs with a loaded weight of 39,500lbs.

M1133 Medical Evacuation Vehicle (MEV)

Unarmed MEVs are assigned to battalion and company levels for protected medical evacuation. Using a Stryker for this purpose allows the evacuation vehicle to keep up with the unit and evacuate casualties over rough terrain.

A: M1126 Infantry Carrier Vehicle (ICV)

B1: M1129A Mortar Carrier (MC-A)

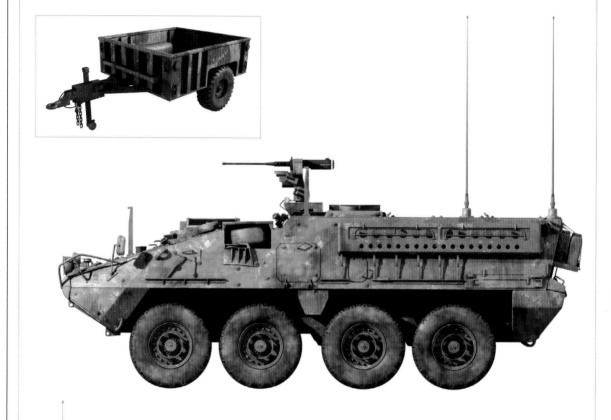

B2: M1129B Mortar Carrier (MC-B)

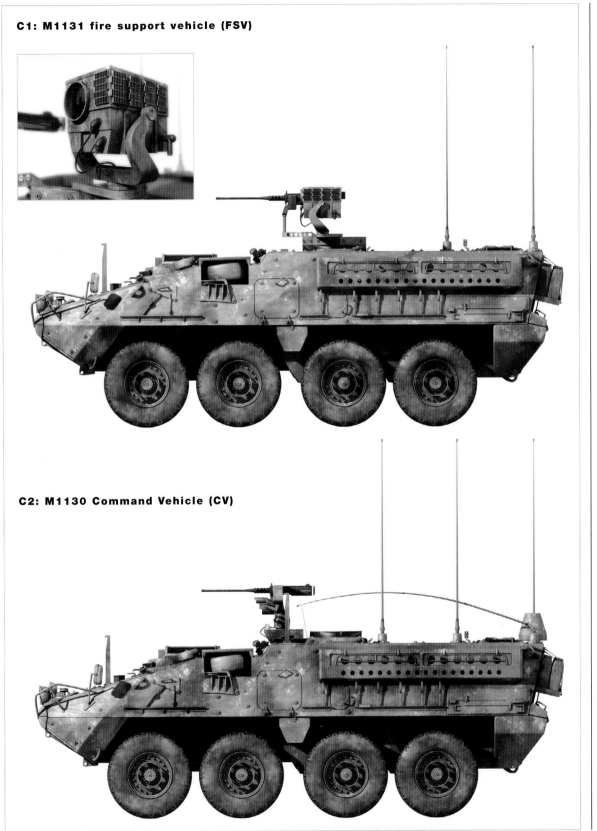

C1: M1131 fire support vehicle (FSV)

C2: M1130 Command Vehicle (CV)

D: M1126 INFANTRY CARRIER VEHICLE

KEY

1 Self-recovery Rotzler Treibmatic powered winch
2 Allison MD 3066P automatic transmission
3 Driver's compartment
4 Michelin 1200R20 XML tires with Hutchinson run-flat liners
5 Mechron 28.5-volt DC auxiliary power unit
6 Delphi air conditioner (optional; standard on CV)
7 Caterpillar 3126 350hp diesel engine
8 Side "bail-out" hatch
9 Squad leader's viewer monitor
10 Squad leader's top hatch
11 Vehicle commander's hatch with seven M45 periscopes
12 TRW Command, Control, Communications, Computer, Intelligence, Surveillance, and Reconnaissance (C4ISR) system

13 XM151 Remote Weapons Station mounting .50cal. M2 machine gun (40mm Mk 19 Mod 3 automatic grenade launcher, alternative)
14 Four M6 smoke grenade dischargers
15 Two fuel tank sponsons (left and right), 53gal (200.5 liters) total capacity
16 Dual spectrum fire suppression systems (also in engine compartment)
17 Rear drop ramp with inset troop hatch
18 Overhead "air-guard" hatches (two)

E1: M1132 Engineer Squad Vehicle (ESV)

E2: M1133 Medical Evacuation Vehicle (MEV)

F1: M1134 Antitank Guided Missile Vehicle (ATGM)

F2: M1128 Mobile Gun System (MGS)

G: M1126 ICV with slat armor

G

Besides the two-man crew it has a trauma specialist, and four litter or six sitting or two litter and three sitting patients can be carried. The right three-quarters of the casualty compartment behind the commander's hatch is built-up 10in and the overall compartment is wider. The MEV weighs 37,930lbs with a loaded weight of 38,570lbs.

M1134 Antitank Guided Missile Vehicle (ATGM)

The ATGM Stryker is employed as an antiarmor and assault weapon. It mounts a GDLS remote TOW turret above the center of the rear compartment. This has two TOW 2B missile tubes with a thermal imager and day video camera, all in an armored pod and capable of being elevated to 20in. It can be rotated 360 degrees with a target tracking rate of 15 degrees per second. The pod can be angled upwards 29 degrees and depressed 20 degrees. It is operated from within the vehicle, but a loader must expose himself to reload, a process that takes two minutes. The ATGM has a four-man crew. There are four four-tube M6 grenade launchers mounted on the launcher housing, and a M240B machine gun is mounted forward of the commander's hatch or a .50cal. on a cupola. The ATGM weighs 39,980lbs with a loaded weight of 40,920lbs. It serves as a surrogate vehicle for the MGS and is provided with bunker-buster missiles as well as antiarmor missiles. The bunker-buster can blow a 24in hole through over 8in of reinforced concrete and demolish heavily constructed sandbag and timber bunkers, while the antiarmor missile can destroy any tank made. The TOW 2B missiles have a 3,750m range.

M1135 NBC Reconnaissance Vehicle (NBCRV)

Owing to developmental problems, the NBCRV was not fielded until 2006. It is fitted with an overpressure system that maintains a higher internal air pressure than exterior air pressure to prevent NBC agents from infiltrating the vehicle. This allows the four-man crew to operate without protective suits and masks. An integrated NBC sensor suite and meteorological system include the joint service standoff chemical agent detector and M21 remote sensing chemical agent alarm. Soil, water, and air samples may be collected and tape and flags can be dispersed to mark contaminated areas and by-pass routes. The rear ramp is replaced by a

A TOW 2 missile is launched from this M1134 Antitank Guided Missile Vehicle (ATGM). The launcher pod is elevated 20in for firing. This ATGM is fitted with MEXAS 2 ceramic appliqué armor tiles. Note the gap in the appliqué tiles for the engine air intake and side hatch. (GDLS)

housing for NBC sample collection means and various sensor masts are fitted on the top deck; the rear compartment has also been widened. The NBCRV's armament is a RWS with a .50cal. The 6x6 M93A1 NBC reconnaissance system is used in lieu of the M1135.

CONTROVERSY

The Stryker is arguably the most controversial AFV ever to enter the US Army inventory, the dispute far surpassing the development of the Bradley IFV some 30 years earlier. Within some circles the debate has become

The M1131 Fire Support Vehicle (FSV) mounts a Fire Support Sensor System (FS3) to the left of the vehicle commander's hatch. This FSV has a 40mm automatic grenade launcher on the vehicle commander's cupola, but they usually mount a .50cal. Six M6 smoke grenade launchers are mounted over the side "bailout" hatch. (GDLS)

A squad of Company B, 4th Battalion, 23d Infantry Regiment, 172d Infantry Brigade (Separate), the third SBCT converted, conduct training in Alaska. The man in the foreground is armed with a 12ga Mossberg 590 pump-action shotgun in addition to his 5.56mm M4 carbine. (US Army)

emotional and even hateful. There are a number of issues concerning the Stryker that many feel make it, and for that matter, any wheeled AFV, a less than prudent choice, including:

- Inadequate armor protection from medium-caliber guns, ATGMs, RPGs, and other antiarmor weapons.
- Inadequate underside protection from mines.
- Too heavy and too much pre-loading preparation for transport in a C-130.
- Insufficient testing during the short development period.
- Too top heavy with a roll-over hazard.
- Too high a profile.
- Weight and maneuverability problems caused by the slat armor.
- Inadequate armament capable of defeating enemy APCs, field fortifications, and defended buildings.[8]
- Insufficient interior room for passengers and equipment.
- Non-stabilized armament does not allow accurate fire while moving.
- Lack of vision ports/periscopes, denying passengers situational awareness.
- Lack of firing ports for passenger weapons.
- Inadequate vision for the vehicle commander and squad leader.
- Commander/gunner forced to expose himself to reload and clear jammed main weapon.
- Overheating of computer and other electronics.
- Lack of amphibious capability and insufficient fording depth. Entering the water during fording must be at slow speed to prevent flooding the engine compartment.
- Vulnerability of rubber tires to gunfire, fragmentation, and mines.
- Wheeled vehicle's natural inability to negotiate some obstacles.
- Wheeled vehicle's poor mobility in mud, sand, and snow.
- Rapid tire wear-out on rocky desert terrain.
- Excessive fuel consumption; higher than advertised.
- Too expensive for what it provides.
- Escalating costs to correct unforeseen problems and add additional capabilities.
- Higher than forecast operating and maintenance costs.
- Not invented in the United States of America.

Any sophisticated AFV has teething problems. This was no less true of the Stryker, even though it had long been in use worldwide as the Piranha and variants. There will always be cost overruns and unforeseen problems. These issues, though, were amplified in some ways by having only just over two years of testing and development rather than the typical eight to ten years. Thus, it was recognized from the outset that problems would emerge and that they would have to be fixed as each block of vehicles was procured. After the testing of LAV IIIs, the first Strykers were delivered in February 2002 and were standardized in May.

Making changes during the manufacture of subsequent vehicles and implementing fixes to fielded vehicles has greatly accelerated the

---

8 It was considered mounting the LAV-25 turret with a 25mm gun, but the configuration exceeds weight and height limitations.

The rear housing hatch, similar to that found on the Fox NBC reconnaissance vehicle, is open on this M1135 NBC Reconnaissance Vehicle (NBCRV). This housing contains ground sample collection systems and marker dispersers. Note the NBC airborne sample collection masts atop the vehicle. This NBCRV has experimental appliqué armor. (US Army)

procurement and fielding process. Since the vehicles have been standardized and fielded with operational units the image of a seriously flawed system has been enhanced. Problems are corrected as soon as possible, including the following modifications recommended by soldiers:

- Replace civilian automobile-type seat belts with a more quickly fastened and released aircraft-type belt long enough to accommodate body armor.
- Addition of a bench seat in the CV to accommodate more personnel.
- Fitting a driver's viewing monitor in the troop compartment to improve situational awareness.
- To prevent RWS drift when firing, add a brace arm and the operating software to be fixed.
- Gun shields should be tested to protect exposed crewmen.

Ultimately, however, a wheeled AFV does have extensive limitations when compared to a full-tracked counterpart. The heavier full-tracked chassis can support a heavier load (armor and armament), has a lower center of gravity, can negotiate rough terrain and obstacles better, and provides enhanced protection from mines. Tracked AFVs are also more compact because less space is required by the tracks as opposed to large wheel wells, and tracked hulls can be made smaller (28 percent more weight/space efficient). The space required for wheels also gives the vehicle a higher profile and center of gravity. Within days of the Strykers' deployment to Iraq, two rolled over, killing three soldiers and fueling further controversy over the Stryker design.

Many of the arguments outlined above are valid, especially those concerning the extent of protection against RPGs, light armament, no vision/firing ports, no amphibious capability, and poor mobility on rough/difficult ground with bar armor. Fuel consumption was reported as 5–6mpg

The driver's station viewed from the troop compartment's connecting passageway. The seat back has been lowered and the driver's overhead hatch is open. The Stryker has power-steering and an automatic transmission. (GDLS)

This ATGM has its TOW launcher pod lowered to the travel position. Normally four M6 smoke grenade launchers are mounted on brackets on the right side of the TOW launcher. While not apparent in black-and-white photographs, the vehicle commander's and driver's vision blocks are reddish in color to make them laser eye-safe. (GDLS)

on roads, but it achieves only 2–3mpg in stop-and-go maneuvers on rough terrain and in urban areas. Instead of requiring a refuel every three days it is necessary every two days – this is still better than the 12–18 hours required by an Abrams unit.

The main complaint is that the Stryker simply does not have all of the advantages of a full-tracked AFV. A tracked AFV would be a more effective vehicle, but the overriding reason a wheeled vehicle was adopted was the absolute necessity for a rapidly air-deployable vehicle requiring smaller logistic demands. Yet, the Stryker is border-line on weight limitations.

Cost is another issue. Program costs had increased 22 percent from the estimate in 2000 of $7.1 billion to $8.7 billion in 2003 – the baseline cost for an ICV is $4 million, $5 million for the MGS, and about $4.5 million for other variants. A Marine LAV-25 costs $900,000. To up-armor a $62,000 HMMWV costs up to $150,000. The contract requirement covers the supply of 2,131 vehicles for $4 billion, the number of vehicles increased from the original 2,096.

After testing and evaluation from May 2002 the Stryker entered operational service in November 2003. Vehicles were contracted in blocks sufficient to equip one SBCT at a time. For example, the fourth SBCT block was contracted in March–June 2004 for delivery in 2005–06 and for the fifth SBCT in February 2005 for 2006–07 delivery.

Congress mandated the Medium Armored Vehicle Comparison Evaluation in September 2002 to evaluate the Stryker against the M113A3 APC,[9] preferred by many. Testing was between four of each AFV. The first SBCT raised undertook training at the National Training Center, Ft. Irwin, CA, followed by an evaluated exercise at the Joint Readiness Training Center, Ft. Polk, LA, and both results were included in the report. The brigade deployed by air, land, and sea to Ft. Polk with 1,500 vehicles, including 293 Strykers. The Secretary of Defense reported the results to Congress concluding, "Current design and training performance of the first SBCT meets the requirements of the Organizational and Operational Concept." This satisfied few, with many claiming a whitewash. Regardless, SBCTs have been organized, equipped, trained, and employed in combat.

---

9 Some civilian groups encourage that the M113 be called the "Gavin;" this is not an official designation.

STRYKER BRIGADE COMBAT TEAMS

In October 1999 General Shinseki announced that two technology-enhanced, fast-deployable, and lethal brigades would be activated on the basis of knowledge gleaned from Force XXI experiments and using off-the-shelf technology. In November 2001 the Department of Defense approved the six planned SBCTs. At one time up to eight SBCTs were considered, but the need was reassessed as six, including one in the National Guard:

1. 3d Brigade, 2d Infantry Division, Ft. Lewis, WA
2. 1st Brigade, 25th Infantry Division (Light), Ft. Lewis, WA
3. 172d Infantry Brigade (Light) (Separate), Ft. Wainwright, AK
4. 2d Cavalry Regiment, Ft. Polk, LA
5. 2d Brigade, 25th Infantry Division (Light), Scholfield Barracks, HI
6. 56th Brigade, 28th Infantry Division (National Guard),
Philadelphia, PA

With the reorganization of divisions into the Modular Force structure, the designations and assignment of the SBCTs will change. Modular Force divisions have four BCTs rather than three. Three of the SBCTs will be located at Ft. Lewis and assigned to the 2d Infantry Division. The division headquarters and one non-Stryker BCT will be in South Korea. The 25th Infantry Division headquartered in Hawaii will have two SBCTs, one in Hawaii itself and one in Alaska. The division's other two brigades include a non-Stryker BCT in Hawaii and an airborne BCT in Alaska. The 2d Cavalry Regiment, formally the 2d Armored Cavalry Regiment (Light) at Ft. Polk, LA, was to have been transferred to Ft. Lewis for conversion, but will now be assigned to Germany, eventually as the only combat maneuver unit stationed there. The assets of the 2d Cavalry will apparently be re-flagged as the 3d SBCT, 2d Division, at Ft. Lewis while the 3d BCT, 3d Infantry Division, will provide the assets of the new 2d Cavalry. While still designated 2d Cavalry Regiment for traditional reasons, it will be organized as a SBCT. It is not clear how these changes will affect the National Guard SBCT.

The M1133 Medical Evacuation Vehicle (MEV) is unarmed. The heightened and widened casualty compartment is evident. It is the only Stryker with a heightened rear compartment, although the MC-B and NBCRV have similar widened structures. (US Army)

A Stryker rifle platoon's four ICVs head out on a mounted patrol. (US Army)

The first SBCT, 3d Brigade, 2d Infantry Division, began Stryker conversion in July 2000 and completed in April 2003. After extensive training and testing it deployed to Iraq in November 2003 and redeployed home in November 2004. It was followed by the second SBCT, 1st Brigade, 25th Infantry Division, which began conversion in April 2003 and completed in June 2004. It deployed to Iraq in September. The 172d Infantry Brigade (Separate) began its conversion in July 2004 and completed in July 2005.

In March 2005 the 2d Cavalry Regiment began conversion and was scheduled for completion in February 2006. Initially it was going to be organized differently to other SBCTs and was still tasked as the XVIII Airborne Corps' reconnaissance unit. It now appears that it will be organized as a SBCT in Germany and the schedule may change. The 2d Brigade, 25th Infantry Division, was planned to convert in March 2006 and complete in February 2007. The National Guard 56th Brigade, 28th Infantry Division, will convert at an earlier date than scheduled. Plans now call for a seventh SBCT for the 2d Infantry Division in 2007.

The SBCT combines the capacity for rapid deployment with survivability and tactical mobility, and a state-of-the-art C4ISR system. The Stryker enables the SBCT to maneuver in confined and urban terrain, provides protection in open terrain, and transports infantry quickly to critical battlefield positions. The SBCT is described as a full-spectrum operations capable, infantry-centric combat force intended to fill the capability gap between heavy and light forces. It is designed to provide balanced lethality, mobility, and survivability optimized for commitment to smaller-scale contingency operations.

The brigades were initially designated as Interim Brigade Combat Teams (IBCT) or "medium brigades." SBCTs are being converted from existing brigades of various types and are an entirely new type of unit with capabilities not possessed by any other. When the IBCT was announced officials emphasized that it was not an experimental force, but a combat-deployable unit once fielded. It will cost $12 billion to field the six SBCTs. Fuel, maintenance, and parts costs are about 25 percent less than the operating costs of a heavy BCT and require 700 fewer troops.

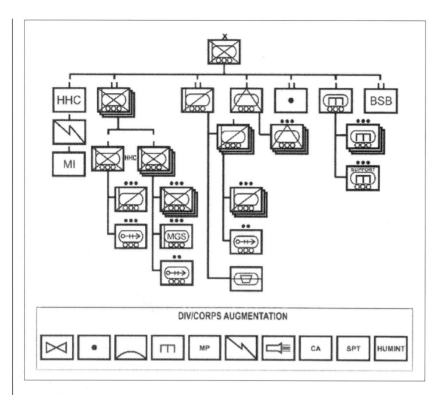

The SBCT may be assigned to an infantry division or act as a separate unit. The two divisions to which they are assigned have two or three SBCTs and one or two non-Stryker BCTs. A SBCT is comprised of a brigade headquarters and headquarters company, signal, military intelligence, anti-tank, and engineer combat companies, three Stryker infantry battalions, a RSTA cavalry squadron, a field artillery battalion (headquarters and service battery, three towed howitzer batteries [4 x 155mm], target acquisition platoon), and a brigade support battalion (headquarters, supply distribution, forward maintenance, and medical support companies). SBCT strength is 3,813 soldiers. A digital brigade detachment provides digital connection with higher headquarters not yet possessing comparable communications. Combat support and service support elements may be attached from division or corps as required for the mission.

The Stryker infantry battalion has a headquarters and headquarters company with command, company headquarters, staff, and communications sections plus reconnaissance (4 x RV), mortar (4 x MC, 4 x 120mm, 4 x 81mm), and medical platoons. The three rifle companies are extremely robust compared to their counterparts in other units. Besides the headquarters (2 x ICV) there is a mobile gun platoon (3 x MGS), a mortar section (2 x MC), a two-man sniper team (1 x 7.62mm M24, 1 x .50cal. XM107), and a medical evacuation team (1 x MEV). The three rifle platoons have a four-man platoon headquarters, three nine-man rifle squads, a seven-man machine-gun squad, and the seven-man mounted element (4 x ICV). Individual weapons arming the rifle squad include 7 x 5.56mm M4 carbines, 2 x 40mm M203A1 grenade launchers (mounted on M4s), 2 x 5.56mm M249 squad automatic weapons (SAW), and a Javelin M98A1 advanced antitank system. The platoon's machine-gun squad possesses 2 x 7.62mm M240B light machine guns. The mounted element

An ATGM vehicle commander scans for targets with a 7.62mm M240B machine gun. Another crewman searches for targets from a rear "air-guard" hatch. The four M6 smoke grenade launchers are evident. (US Army)

has four drivers and three vehicle commanders; the platoon sergeant doubles as the machine-gun squad's vehicle commander.

The cavalry squadron has a headquarters and a headquarters troop,[10] three reconnaissance troops, and a surveillance troop. Recon troops have a headquarters, a mortar section (2 x MC, 2 x 120mm), and three recon platoons (4 x RC). The surveillance troop possesses four ground surveillance radars, three RQ-7 Shadow unmanned aerial vehicles, and radio intercept and direction-finding equipment.

The Stryker rifle company's mobile gun platoon will be equipped with three MGS vehicles. From 2001 the test units were equipped with a variety of "surrogate" vehicles including HMMWVs mounting TOW missiles, Italian 105mm gun-armed Centauro B1 armored cars, M113A3 APCs with dismountable M220A2 TOWs, and improved TOW acquisition systems (ITAS) mounted on HMMWVs. Until the MGS is available the TOW-armed ATGM will equip this platoon.

Another substitute is for the NBCRV. The M93A1 Fox NBC reconnaissance system is currently being used and the German-designed TPZ1 Fuchs has also been in use with the US Army since 1990. The NBCRV will eventually replace the Fox throughout the Army.

The SBCT has 293 Strykers with 108 x ICV, 48 x RV, 36 x MC, 9 x ESV, 25 x CV, 12 x FSV, 9 x ATGM, 16 x MEV, 27 x MGS, and 3 x NBCRV. Weaponry includes 121 x Javelin M93A1 AT launchers, 12 x 155mm M198 howitzers (to be replaced by M777A1 weapons from late 2006), 36 x 120mm M120 mortars, 12 x 81mm M252 mortars, and 18 x 60mm M224 mortars.

---

10 In US service the squadron is a battalion-size unit and the troop is company-size.

COMBAT DEBUT

The Stryker entered operational service with the US Army when the 3d Brigade, 2d Infantry Division, landed in Kuwait in November 2002 with 309 Strykers and deployed into northern Iraq, where it operated until November 2004. The first SBCT was assigned to the area around Mosul and the 5,000-man brigade relieved the 101st Airborne Division (Air Assault), a force three times larger than the brigade now responsible for a 36,246 sq km (14,000 sq mile) area.

As mentioned previously, the problems of the Stryker are manifold and controversial. The MGS is urgently needed, as the ATGM's TOW missiles are not effective against fleeting insurgent targets. Because of the extent of patrol and escort missions, ATGMs and MCs, for example, are used alongside ICVs and RVs.

As already noted, the major threat to the Stryker and all other vehicles in theater is the RPG-7. In training exercises, the Army has not effectively replicated this flexible weapon's capabilities or its unconventional tactical use. The Abrams is mostly impervious to the RPG and the Bradley only less so. Anything else is vulnerable, including the Stryker. Other threats include improvised explosive devices (IEDs) ranging from roadside-emplaced artillery rounds to massive buried bombs and car bombs (parked command-detonated and suicide) able to destroy an Abrams.

SBCTs in Iraq have lost Strykers, but although small numbers have been totally destroyed, the majority have been repaired. A rebuild facility was established in Qatar in the summer of 2005 to refurbish battle-damaged Strykers and return them to Iraq. This facility prevents vehicles destined for new brigades from being used as replacements. Overall the extent of damage and casualties suffered by Stryker units has been comparatively light.

An overhead view of an ICV shows the arrangement of the slat armor. The squad leader's hatch is seen to the left of the vehicle commander's hatch. Riflemen occupy the rear "air-guard" hatches. The black fabric rolls are Kevlar® fragmentation/bomb blankets. It is recommended that sandbags not be used for additional protection with slat armor because of the added weight, but nonetheless they are still employed. (US Army)

An example of a RPG attack occurred in March 2004. Two RPGs struck an ICV, igniting externally stowed fuel cans. Ammunition that was also stowed externally cooked off and the vehicle burned, but the troops escaped. One Stryker was rolled one-and-a-half times by a 500lb car bomb. The crew was uninjured and when it was rolled upright the vehicle was drivable. Attacks such as these, and the rumor that high command ordered that Strykers not be committed to Fallujah and Najaf in early 2005 for fear of excessive losses, have fueled doubts about the vehicle. However, the actual reason for the caution was that the green 1st Brigade, 25th Infantry Division, had been in-country less than a month and it was not considered ready for such action.

In December 2003 an ICV was destroyed by a fire in the engine compartment caused by a large buried IED near Samarra. One crewman was injured and the rest maintain they would have all been casualties if in an HMMWV. During an attack in October 2004 in Mosul an ICV was rammed by a suicide car bomb, resulting in heavy damage. The commander was killed and seven of the tires damaged, but the Stryker was able to return to its base with the rest of the crew unharmed. In October a Bradley was struck by a car bomb, while in December a Stryker was similarly hit. Both lost their forward suspension arm, but only the Stryker retained its mobility.

The observations of Lieutenant Colonel Michael E. Kurilla commanding 3d Battalion, 24th Infantry, 1st Brigade, 25th Infantry Division, sum up the realities of the Stryker's combat effectiveness. His battalion served in Mosul from October 2004. He took exception to accusations that the Stryker's survivability and maintenance were substandard and threatened soldiers' lives. In its first six months his unit was subjected 186 RPG attacks, 122 IEDs, and 33 car bombs (ten were suicide cars), as well as extensive small-arms and mortar attacks. Car bombs are the most dangerous to Strykers, with most carrying around 500lbs of explosives – Kurilla saw four make direct contact with Strykers and detonate. In the ten suicide car attacks a number of soldiers were wounded, but none lost a limb or were killed. A suicide truck bomb detonated with 2,000lbs of explosives only 25m from a Stryker without knocking it out. The colonel cites one particular Stryker hit by eight RPGs, nine IEDs, and a car bomb plus countless small-arms rounds. Six of the squad suffered light wounds and remained in Iraq. Stryker C21 remained operational or in a couple instances was repaired within 24 hours. The battalion suffered casualties while conducting dismounted operations and not while in Strykers.

The colonel also describes an ambush on a reconnaissance platoon by 50–65 insurgents. They fired at least 100 RPGs at the four Strykers and also employed IEDs and small arms. All of the Strykers took multiple hits and continued to fight and maneuver. Only a few men were wounded.

The Strykers averaged 1,600km (1,000 miles) a month and already had many miles on them upon deployment. The 75 vehicles also averaged 96 percent or better operational readiness – only three or four were down at any given time. The same applied to computers, cameras, and other electronic systems. No other Army AFV has had such a high operational rate. Most damaged vehicles were back on the streets within 24 hours. Kurilla maintains:

> In urban combat, there is no better vehicle for delivering a squad of infantrymen to close with and destroy the enemy. It is fast, quiet, incredibly survivable, reliable, lethal, and capable of providing amazing situational awareness.

The US Army is aware that the Stryker is not perfect and requires many fixes, and modifications are underway. The M1 Abrams itself has undergone five major modifications and countless minor fixes. For all its faults the Stryker provides significantly more protection than the up-armored HMMWV. It is questionable if the M113A3 would be a better vehicle. It has advantages in some areas and weaknesses in others. One of the main points many soldiers in Iraq make is that the M113 is not fast enough nor has the rapid acceleration of the up-armored HMMWV or Stryker. They prefer the ability to dash at high speed and credit that capability as more critical than armor in order to survive IED and RPG attacks.

Regardless of its shortfalls the Stryker will remain in the inventory for some time, probably at least another 15–20 years.

BIBLIOGRAPHY

Foss, Christopher F., *Jane's Armour & Artillery, 2004–2005* (Coulsdon, UK: Jane's Information Group, 2004)

Hunnicutt, R. P., *Armored Car: A History of American Wheeled Combat Vehicles* (Novato, CA: Presidio, 2002) – does not include the Stryker

Vick, Alan; Orletsky, David; Pirnie, Bruce; and Jones, Seth, *The Stryker Brigade Combat Team: Rethinking Strategic Responsiveness and Assessing Deployment Options* (Santa Monica, CA: RAND Corporation, 2002)

US Army Field Manuals

The SBCT Infantry Rifle Platoon and Squad, FM 3-21.9, December 2002

The SBCT Infantry Rifle Company, FM 3-21.11, October 2002

The Stryker Brigade Combat Team Infantry Battalion, FM 3-21.21, April 2003

The Stryker Brigade Combat Team, FM 3-21.31, March 2003

COLOR PLATE COMMENTARY

Note: Comparison of prototype vehicles and vehicles from different production blocks will reveal many minor differences in fittings and their arrangement, weapon and sensor mountings, and on-vehicle equipment. Left and right orientations are in reference to the vehicle's left and right and not the viewer's.

A: M1126 INFANTRY CARRIER VEHICLE (ICV)

This left front view of the ICV exhibits the basic Stryker used as the foundation for most other variants. This one mounts a 40mm Mk 19 Mod 3 automatic grenade launcher on the XM151 Remote Weapons Station (RWS). Its ammunition container holds 32 rounds. Of a rifle platoon's four Strykers, two mount 40mm weapons and two .50cal. M2 machine guns. Four four-tube M6 smoke grenade launchers are fitted to the RWS. The squad leader's hatch is to the left of the vehicle commander's hatch and the bailout hatch is on the side below it. On-board tools include two shovels, pick, axe, and pry bar. The right rear view (see plate D) displays the rear ramp with its inset troop hatch and the two rear "air-guard" hatches. The external fuel sponsons are on the bottom sides of the hull on either side of the ramp. Two 5gal (approx. 20 liters) fuel and two 5gal water cans are standard issue for rear mounting.

B1: M1129A MORTAR CARRIER (MC-A)

The MC-A is essentially an IFV with internal stowage racks for a 120mm M120 and either an 81mm M252 or 60mm M224 mortar, as well as stowage for ammunition. The mortars must be dismounted to fire.

B2: M1129B MORTAR CARRIER (MC-B)

The MC-B is provided with a two-section top hatch providing the turntable-mounted 120mm M121 mortar a 360-degree rotation. As with the MC-A, a storage rack for either an 81mm M252 or 60mm M224 mortar is provided. The 120mm can be dismounted for ground firing, for which a bipod and base plate are carried. The MC is provided with a two-wheel 1 1/2-ton M1102 LTT-H for ammunition and crew equipment. The trailer (shown here as an inset) is provided with bows and a forest green or desert tan vinyl-canvas cover (not shown). The trailer tires are the same as used on the HMMWV.

ABOVE **A close-up of the frontal slat armor of an ICV. A spare tire was originally planned to be carried on the rear ramp, but this interfered with the inset troop door. Spares are seldom carried, but can be located either on the rear top deck forward of the "air-guard" hatches or just behind the driver's hatch as here. (US Army)**

LEFT **Strykers, although deployed in Iraq, have retained their lusterless green paint. A coating of dust makes them appear to be painted in desert sand color. Note the concertina wire coils stowed behind the slat armor. (US Army)**

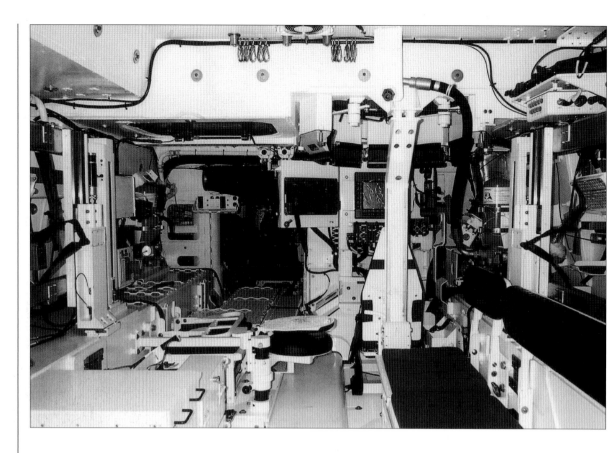

The interior, looking forward, of the Stryker Command Vehicle (CV). The commander's station is to the right and the passageway to the driver's station is to the left. A closed overhead hatch is seen above the passageway. The inside of all hatches are lusterless green, the same as the vehicle's exterior. (GDLS)

C1: M1131 FIRE SUPPORT VEHICLE (FSV)
The FSV's main "armament" is an array of sensors and targeting devices in the form of the Fire Support Sensor System (FS3). The M1135 Reconnaissance Vehicle (RV) is identical externally, but the Long-Range Advanced Scout Surveillance System (LRAS3) with an array of sensors (see inset) replaces the FS3 beside the commander's hatch. Both vehicles are armed with a .50cal. machine gun.

C2: M1130 COMMAND VEHICLE (CV)
The CV is armed with a .50cal. machine gun on a RWS. Depending on the echelon of unit it supports, the CV can mount three to five radios in addition to portable radios for dismounted use.

D: M1126 INFANTRY CARRIER VEHICLE
This cutaway view of the ICV focuses on the troop compartment in which the nine-man rifle squad is carried. Numerous storage racks and containers are provided and ammunition is stowed beneath the lift-up bench seats. While the compartment is not overly crowded, there is little extra space. It is necessary for squad and crew rucksacks to be carried on the vehicle's exterior side stowage racks – this exposes their gear to rain, dust, and enemy fire, and there is a danger of the rucksacks being torn off when traveling through dense vegetation or confined urban streets. The vehicle was not designed to carry a spare tire, but in combat one is often kept on the rear deck.

E1: M1132 ENGINEER SQUAD VEHICLE (ESV)
The ESV is a modified ICV. It is normally fitted with a mine-plow, which can also be used to clear light obstacles and rubble, but this can be replaced by a mine-roller. Both are made by Pearson Engineering of Britain. Flag racks to mark cleared lanes can be seen on the back. The ESV is armed with a .50cal. machine gun on a RWS.

E2: M1133 MEDICAL EVACUATION VEHICLE (MEV)
The heightened and widened casualty compartment is apparent on the MEV. The Geneva crosses are displayed on sheet-metal plates that can be folded in half for concealment or in the event that the enemy chooses not to honor civilized conventions, the same reason medics are armed, allowing them to protect their patients and themselves. The MEV itself is unarmed.

F1: M1134 ANTITANK GUIDED MISSILE VEHICLE (ATGM)
The ATGM's twin-tube TOW launcher pod is shown elevated to full firing height. It can be lowered to where its bottom rests on the deck. Early versions had two M6 smoke grenade launchers; current models have four. Armament is a 7.62mm M240B machine gun.

F2: M1128 MOBILE GUN SYSTEM (MGS)

Numerous turret designs and gun housings are seen on prototype MGS vehicles as efforts were made to reduce its weight and height. A .50cal. machine gun is mounted on the right side of the turret and a 7.62mm coaxial machine gun to the above left of the main gun. A major cause of the MGS' overweight problems is the automatic reloader – it holds 18 rounds with eight rounds in the carousel and ten in the replenishment rack.

G: M1126 ICV WITH SLAT ARMOR

All Strykers deployed to Iraq have been fitted with slat armor as a stop-gap means of protection from RPG-7 attacks in lieu of the original defective ceramic armor tiles. The armor adds 5,200lbs to the vehicle's weight and 12–14in width on each side. This weight affects its dash speed and maneuverability in confined built-up areas (two Strykers often cannot pass one another on many streets), and has caused roll-overs. It over-stresses the suspension system and the vehicles cannot be carried in aircraft with the armor mounted. To cope with the weight, the tires are inflated to 90lbs per square inch and the central tire inflation system is disconnected – if the tire pressure is reduced when the vehicle leaves a road the weight will prevent the tires from being re-inflated once it regains a road. Vehicles venturing off-road have had to be winched out of soft ground. Slat armor reduces the number of fuel/water cans from 20 to 16 because of mounting brackets. While the rear ramp can be lowered, the ramp's troop door and the left side bailout hatch cannot be used. This ICV's RWS is fitted with a .50cal. M2 and its 200-round ammunition container.

ABOVE **This mine-plow equipped Engineer Squad Vehicle (ESV) at the National Training Center is towing an M58A1 Mine-Clearing Line Charge (MICLIC). It launches a 107m linear charge containing 1,840lbs of C-4 explosives and can blast a 14m wide, 100m long gap through a minefield. (US Army)**

BELOW **The XM151 RWS mounting a .50cal. M2 machine gun and four four-tube M6 smoke grenade launchers. A 40mm Mk 19 Mod 3 automatic grenade launcher may be substituted. The RWS is not stabilized, thus preventing effective fire on the move, but this deficiency is due for correction. (US Army)**

INDEX